LETTERS *To An* INCARCERATED *Sista*

SABRINA POWELL

Letters To An Incarcerated Sista

Copyright© 2022 Sabrina Powell

ISBN: 978-1-956884-06-7

Contributing Editor: or all services completed by Imprint Productions, Inc.
Cover Design: or all services completed by Imprint Productions, Inc.

Printed in the United States of America
Published by Imprint Productions, Inc.
First Edition 2022

LETTERS *To An* INCARCERATED *Sista*

I want to acknowledge family and friends for their support and feedback known and unknown in this creation of mine. A special thank you to ImPrint Productions for helping me bring my vision to life and Carter & Carter Productions for the first of many photographs. *Peace and Blessings.*

INTRODUCTION

Hey love, let me start by saying the letters you are about to read come filled with love and the compassion of a sister, mother, or the voice you hear inside when filled with doubt. My sisters, I want you to know that there are different forms of incarceration: mental, physical, and spiritually bound. So when you feel stuck or a dark space filling up around or inside you, open up this book and let your mind and spirit be filled with ease and "Just know that whatever you are going through, it is just a "minor setback for a major comeback." - *Cidney Watson*

This came to me while I was reading quotes, and I thought about how I was when I was incarcerated and at times wished I had letters from someone that had been through what I had been through. I would have wanted that person to let me know that even though I am here

7

right now it is just for a season and just like the weather it will change you, I just have to know in your heart that it will, and once you know this, things start to change. Sometimes you can see it and other times it will get messy before it gets better, it's called "being blessed in the midst of the mess." When this happens, you know that a blessing has happened, but you really don't realize it until all the chaos has calmed down and you have a minute to think back, slow down, and look at what you have come through. Then and only then will you see the blessings you have asked God for or whoever your higher power is in your life.

SELF

My sisters, when you are going through anything in this life, no matter how difficult, there is always a force bigger than you that keeps you pushing through to another day. The reason these things have happened to you is because there is going to be a blessing, a really big blessing, when your storm has passed. So, know that this life is not a race, but it's a marathon and it's going to be some good days and some not so good days but as long as you wake up to face another day, those issues are "a small thing to a giant." You are a powerful young woman who can and will beat any obstacle that comes your way. You want to know why? Because God built you for this and your victory will be the encouragement others need to overcome and walk through their valley.

Heyy love,

Today will be the day that your mind changes and you see things differently than yesterday and know that this day will be blessed and full of things to come. I know that everything seems like it is coming at you so fast, but know that no matter how today looks, tomorrow is a new bright and sunny day. So, STOP feeling ashamed of how many times you have fallen, and start being proud of how many times you have gotten up, dusted yourself off, and tried again. (We are far from perfect). So never be ashamed of who you are or what you had to go through to get to where you are now. I want you to know that you are AMAZING, even when you are walking through the darkness.

Good day my Queen,

This is a great and wonderful day to change the way you are thinking today, and not base your outcome on thoughts of yesterday. I want you to remember this: "If you must look back, do so forgivingly. If you must look forward, do so prayerfully. However, the wisest thing you can do is be present in the present... Gratefully" -Maya Angelou

Love, never let your thoughts get the best of you, you are meant to be great, no matter how long it takes or what the naysayers say. Remember this, "It's never how you start baby it's how you finish, so do it with a big smile and with grace." -Sabrina Powell

Heyy love bug,

Today is a day for healing and transformation of your mind. The first thing you need to do today is look yourself in the mirror and say, "I love myself too much to stay the same, today I choose to take it one day at a time, and I'm going to love me starting today!!" I want you to know that when you start to put yourself first, everything else will fall into place. It will be hard some days, but you can do it!! So, when you feel like you want to go to a dark place in your mind, just look in the mirror and smile, knowing that a "queen's crown may get crooked but baby it never falls all the way off!!"

Great day honey,

Today is just a take it all in and relax; sip some tea, lemon water, or something that relaxes you and think about the things you are learning about the new you and what you want to continue to work on and know that this journey is not a race but a marathon. So today do these things: validate yourself, love yourself; motivate yourself; and push yourself. Give to yourself and speak nothing but positive words over yourself and you will heal in places you never thought you would. Today and everyday recommit yourself to yourself. Now if you feel like you are being a little selfish, don't!! We always need a day to reboot and re-energize our mind and body to get our peace and keep our vibes at an all-time high. Therefore, listen to some soft music, take a walk and just be one with yourself. Let all the cares of the day go away and just be you, and when you're done, take a few minutes to write yourself a love note to let yourself know just how much you love you.

Heyy beautiful!!

Yes you. I want you to know that YOU ARE AMAZING, JUST THE WAY YOU ARE. Look at yourself (your body) and take in every part of you; every dimple, wrinkle, stretch mark, all of it and love the skin you're in, because You are the only one in this particular skin. You are the only one on Earth that looks like you or has the ability to be the person that you are. God made you exactly the way you are supposed to be. Today, love who you are and what you look like; oil up that skin, take that picture that you were too afraid to take and live in this moment of loving you.

Heyy girl Heyy!!

Today is a blessed and wonderful day. Right now, as you look at yourself, wrap your arms around yourself and say, "Damn Girl!! you look and feel amazing, and today is going to be a fantabulous day!!." Today, take the time to make 10 people smile, share one good thing about yourself, and when you think no one is watching, burst out into a song that makes you happy. (Now you know someone Is always watching). My favorite has always been, She's a brick house, she's mighty-mighty, just lettin' it all hang out!! Me and my best friend have always been just that in our minds, Brick Houses. And who can tell us differently? That's right nobody, so spend time today smiling and making someone else smile and laugh. It can and will change how your day and someone else's will be. Think about you and your best friend's favorite song and do your jig girl!!

WARRIOR WOMAN

My strong sisters, these next letters will focus on being and finding your inner strength. Now we all are strong in our own way and some of us are stronger than others and that is ok. See with strength, you never really know you have it when it's all you ever had. So with these letters, see where your strength lives and let it blossom into the power you need to move forward and help you overcome the things you thought you never would. Truth be told, honey, you already overcame that too!!

Great day love,

Today is day one of Warrior Woman Week. Let's start today with this quote right here from a book I love titled, 'Warrior Goddess Training' by Heather Ash Amara. This is so true, "No matter what you do, someone will have something negative to say." Now this is the hard part, not to take it personally. This is one of the first lessons of being a warrior woman. See It's not the people in the street that hurt us the most with their words. It's the ones we hold close to us, our significant others, family members, and friends. So when these words that they say hurt you and make you feel uneasy, remember this, "people judge and criticize other people's lives when they're not happy with their own." - Lori Deschene.

This is just like the old saying, hurt people hurt people, so your only goal when it comes to these people is to say, "I choose to put myself first today and every day and how ever you feel about me has nothing to do with me, but everything to do with you. I'm healing. What about you?"

Heyy girl, Heyy

Today is day two of being a Warrior Woman. Today, we are going to write a letter to our fifteen-year-old selves, telling her everything. You be real (tell your darkest secrets) and don't forget to tell her how things are different and what you have learned and what you want her to do differently in her life, and when you are done have a friend do the same thing and y'all switch letters and read them out loud to each other. Now you are asking why would I do this? This is for healing that little girl inside of us that we felt was missing something or was hurt in some way. Because when we heal her, we heal the grown woman we are today. "BECAUSE A HEALED WOMAN IS A STRONGER WOMAN AND A STRONGER WOMAN IS A WARRIOR WOMAN!!"

Heyy girl,

Today is day three of being a Warrior Woman. This quote is so powerful, and I use this one myself. "Those people who tried to bury you, didn't know you were a seed." See people tend to think when they put you in a corner or believe you only have them to depend on, that you can't make it without them. Oh baby, but God!! What the devil meant for your downfall, God will turn it around for your good!! Just because you were being still that didn't mean you weren't growing, exactly what a seed does when it's in the dirt. This time that you are in now might be dark, but the best things come out of dark places. So feed yourself and nourish your mind, so when it's time to blossom, you are full, bright, and able to handle anything that's coming your way.

Good day Warrior Woman,

This is day four, today is the day that you tell the devil this: "You have tried so many times to kill me and you have failed, you have sat me down, knocked me down and I've come back stronger then what I was each time before, so I'm telling you now, you can't have me or my family so stop trying! I have been in your furnace, stood in the midst of your fire and was not burned. Therefore, I tell you, get thee behind me, Satan you will never win!!"

Heyy baby girl,

It's day five of being a Warrior Woman. Today I want you to know that when you tell your story, you are not telling it for people to feel sorry for you. It's to let them know what you have been through, the reason why you may move the way that you do and to let them know you have been hurt and burned, but you made it through. You are a survivor, a warrior, because everyone didn't make it. It takes strength and power greater than yourself to come through trauma, and trauma is anything that leaves an imprint on your mind and spirit. And you can heal them both by talking and writing about it. Always remember your story can always heal and/or inspire someone else.

Heyy love,

Today is day six of being a Warrior Woman. Today I want you to take everything that you have learned this week and use it in your day-to-day life. A warrior woman loves hard, and sometimes it comes with hurt because what you give sometimes is not what you get back. And as a warrior woman that is built from the things that you have been through, know that you owe it to yourself to be with a person who gives you the same amount of love that you give them an even more. Never settle for half of anything, no matter what it is!! You deserve 100% of everything that you ask for because you are a divine spiritual being that has done the healing work within herself to attract the life and the one you want to spend your life with. And one more thing to take with you today and every day: trust your gut, your first mind, your intuition. She will never lead you wrong.

Heyy Warrior Woman,

This is day seven and as we all know it's the number of completion. So I'm going to complete this last Warrior Woman letter with this: Today and every day after this, know that you are the only one that has the power to change anything in your life. You hold the pen to write the chapters of your story, and know that your story can always be rewritten. That's why you are the Warrior Woman you are today because you rewrote the parts of your story that you didn't like and highlighted the parts that made you stronger. Sometimes you don't see that part until you go back and read about what you have been through (thought about them or told someone else) and when you realize that you have made it through, pat yourself on the back and say, "Girl, you did that !!" Then treat yourself to a nice dinner or new outfit, or whatever makes you feel great and you know why? Because you deserve it!! You are a QUEEN!

FEMININITY

This week ladies, we are going to talk about being feminine. Why you might ask? Because some of us are not feminine at all, *myself included, -lol.* Therefore, we will work on our feminine energy this week. Now you might be saying, "I'm feminine, I get my nails done and my hair fixed, I love to wear dresses and heels, and of course I love men." Well love, that's not all that femininity is about, so these letters will be all about embracing everything feminine!

Heyy love bug,

This week is all about Femininity, now this is something that we all as women possess and today, I'm gonna tell you what the real definition of femininity is. (Now when I did my research) everyone said the same thing:

- *Be true to yourself, meaning be comfortable in your own skin. You have to accept yourself as the person you are and never change for anyone. Remember there is nobody else like you. You are it.*

- *Act like you love you, meaning dress yourself in what speaks to you and put your twist on it!! Don't let people, places, and things drain you of your most powerful asset, your energy!! And never let anyone, and I mean anyone, make you feel like you are never good enough, 'CAUSE BABY YOU ARE THE REAL DEAL, PERIODT!!*

- *Be BOLD, be AUTHENTIC, and do what you need to do for you! If you want to go to school, go! If you want to open that*

26

business, do it NOW!! Remember this, always do everything while being attractive in mind, body, and spirit. That's real femininity!! Read Proverbs 31, "The virtuous woman." She's savvy, she takes care of her house, husband, children, is respected by many, and keeps a stream of extra income, etc.

· *Now this is the last thang baby girl, know without a shadow of a doubt, you're IRREPLACEABLE! And that's with any relationship. Know that the only reason you decide to leave is when you feel you need to, and know how valuable you are and what you bring to the table, any table, (YOU!) YOU ARE THE TABLE! Your thoughts, your nurturing, and being open and honest about how you feel about any and everything that's important to you.*

Heyy Girl, Heyy!!!

Today is day two of being feminine. This comes from Billionaire media mogul Oprah Winfrey, she emphasizes, "Think like a queen. A queen is not afraid to fail. Failure is another stepping stone to greatness." What does this have to do with being feminine you ask? As women, we take on challenges and we set goals for ourselves, and sometimes we fall short of the goals we set or a task we took on, but know that failure is all a part of the winning process. And the feminine part is knowing that it doesn't matter what it looks like when you start, it's all about how you finish, with your head held high, full of confidence, and DRESSED TO KILL!

Heyy sweetheart,

It's day three of being feminine, and today we will talk about how to activate that feminine energy and once again, we have it already in us, we just have to wake it up and here's how we start.

- *Connect to your body through movement honey. With this one, the list is endless: Dance, take pole dancing classes, do some kickboxing, go out for a run, etc. It's all about being free in your skin and your spirit.*

- *Allow yourself to receive this, (it's a big one for me) and many other "strong women," remember being strong also means letting people help you when you need it and be confident enough to ask for help when you need it as well. Reflect on the saying, "closed mouths don't get fed," meaning if you never ask, you will never know what you can get.*

- *Listen to your intuition, you will hear me say this a few times, but it's true. My best friends and my momma have always told me this. Now I tell it to my children as well, Trust your (first mind), your intuition. She will never lead you wrong. If she says do more, do more. If she says, don't go, then don't. And when you listen to her, you will never lose!!*

· *Make time for rest, self-care, and beautification.*

· *Ladies, this is the most important step in being feminine and being a woman, PERIODT. We have to rest our mind and body so we can stay at our best. At the top of the list is sleep because it rejuvenates the body and helps it rebuild what has been depleted throughout the day. When it comes to self-care, whatever it means to you, whether it's spa days, getting your hair done, working out, reading books, writing, or whatever it is that you do that brings you peace, DO IT!! Keep yourself and your surroundings beautiful, because when you feel beautiful and look beautiful, you move with more confidence than you ever thought you had!*

· *Activate your senses: You know sight, taste, smell, touch, and hearing, elevating the mind. Look at beautiful things like the sunset or it's rising, excite your taste buds with a great piece of chocolate, ice cream, or anything that you haven't tried. For me, smell is the best of the senses. smelling flowers, foods, perfumes, or Colognes. It is nothing like a great scent, trust me a great scent can take you places and remind you of your favorite times within seconds. Next is hearing, whether it's a soft voice, rhythmic music, even drops of rain can relax you and take away the stresses of the day. So turn on your favorite tune and clean, write or just dance and do whatever you feel!!*

- *Honor your DARK side: Express your emotions to the fullest, but in a safe and positive way. Remember, you are heard more when you speak with a calm voice. Always let your words be seasoned with salt, meaning full of taste to each person that you speak to.*

- *Now, this is a must, honor your sacred sexuality: You must know your body inside and out, know what it looks, smells, and tastes like, and you do this by what you eat and drink. Also, know that when you know yourself, even when it comes to pleasure, no one can tease you and you can tell anyone how to pleasure you as well, and that's something no one can take from you. That's your ULTIMATE FEMININE POWER!! NOW EMBRACE YOUR WILDSIDE!!*

Great day love,

Today is day four of being feminine. Let's start with a quote from a woman who exuded femininity and she said, "There is no force more powerful than a woman determined to rise." -Dorothy Dandridge.

Determination is a thing that no one can take from you. No matter what you have faced in your life. When you overcome your past and become the person you want to be, when everything that was placed in front of you for you to fail and you didn't. Honey, that's power! As I always like to say, "you can never put a limit on determination!!"

Heyy Queen,

Today is day five of being feminine and this QUEEN demanded RESPECT and was very feminine while doing it. Aretha Franklin said, "Be your own artist and always be confident in what you are doing. If you're not going to be confident, you might as well not be doing it". She was femininity personified; she was the only woman to have dress changes at her homegoing, a real DIVA!! I picked her quote for this reason. If you are going to be or do anything in life, trust yourself enough to be the best at whatever it is, and if you don't trust you enough to follow through, don't even attempt to do it until you know you can do it and be the ultimate best at it!

My Queen,

Great day and welcome to day six of being feminine. Today I found a woman that knows the fountain of youth and it's all inside of you!! Miss Sophia Loren stated, "There is a fountain of youth: it is your mind, your talents, the creativity you bring to your life and the lives of the people you love. When you learn to tap this source, you will truly defeat age." I took this as saying your youth, or what keeps you living and full of vitality comes from helping and healing others. What you give to the world, what you create and help bring about the change in another human is what gives you life.

Heyy Babygirl,

Today is a great day and we are on day six of being feminine. Today we will be listing some ways of physically being feminine, and when I tell you it's all in your attitude and then everything else, it really is!! So, as I said at the beginning, you are saying, "I'm feminine, I wear dresses and heels," well now we are at that part, and how to do it. So whatever you want to add is totally up to you boo!! And if you are like me, now that I work all the time, I have to fit in my feminine side. So, when I'm not working, here are some extra things I do and as we are becoming more feminine here are some things we can do.

- *Love the body that you are in! Yep, I said it! Love it! If it's a part of your body that you don't like, dress it up. If you have a big stomach or stretch marks, dress it up, get you some waist beads, body jewelry, high waisted pants, or body shapers when you wear dresses and want to look smoother under your clothes.*

- *Look at your body in the mirror and learn to love every part of it. Inside and out. Talk to her when you are oiling up out of the shower or bath, touch yourself, feel your skin, and take the time to learn her and thank your body for putting up with you. Because when you love and take care of her, she will love and take care of you!!*

· *Get your hair done or do it yourself. Do it however you want to, but make sure it's done and it's in place and flawless. Some older women say don't wear red, Girl Bye!! Put that red on and wear it with pride, it screams out POWER and CONFIDENCE. You should wear it on your nails, lips, and toes (shoes or nail polish)*

· *Wear clothes that flatter your body. Which don't have to be so tight that it hurts, but wear ones that lay on you just right. The ones that show your curves!! pencil skirts, bodycon dresses, now they look like a glove when you put them on but you can move with no problem, and for the women that love to wear jeans like me, choose one that fits you just right. And if they are too big, go and get them tailored to fit, cause WHEN YOU LOOK GOOD, YOU FEEL GOOD!!*

· *Find a scent that you love to wear, and it makes people stop in their tracks, make sure to dab it on your pressure points behind the ears, wrists, neck and spray on your clothes. A SCENT IS WORTH A THOUSAND WORDS!!*

- *Ladies look more natural, I know some of you love your makeup, but trust me, less is more. I like false lashes, so if you're into them, please wear those that are not as long as a bird's wings. Wear the ones that bring your eyes out and apply makeup that's not heavy. If you wear it and always take it off at night, remember to moisturize your face and keep your lips moisturized as well and always smile.*

- *Ladies, remember your hygiene. Stay fresh and clean. Keep you a GIRLY BAG, with an extra outfit because you never know what might happen!! Also have deodorant, underwear, and body wash. Remember to shave and trim the lady parts. Lastly, PLEASE don't forget your toothbrush and toothpaste boo!!*

- *Be sexy at all times. Wear underwear that are sexy but comfortable. Wear a matching bra and panty set when you are out or when you're out on a date, remember being sexy is all about you and how you feel.*

- *Wear jewelry, dress up your wrists and wear rings on every finger. It just speaks GODDESS!! Don't forget to wear toe rings, even if those toes are ugly, dress them up. They are what carry you around. Love on them too!!*

- *Now this is very important. Learn to be the receiver in your relationship. It is ok to give gifts, but you deserve to be loved too!! So, soak up the text messages, phone calls, and the love that is being rained on you, but also send it back out to your mate. Communicating with, loving on, and spending quality time with each other is a must. Please share what you want in and out of your relationship. For the relationship to be successful, you must set and honor each other's boundaries!! Your peace is a must!!!*

Well, ladies,

We have come to the end of the week of being feminine, so I'm going to sum it up with this: Ladies, remember to speak softly and not cuss. Yep, I said it (Baby, God is still working on me. LOL). Let your words be seasoned with salt. Always build up the next sister, a compliment goes a long way. Let a man open a door for you or help carry your heavy boxes. It reminds us to stay in our feminine minds. Speak your mind, follow the beat of your own drum! Own your choices and take accountability for your actions. Remember this, you don't have to spend a lot to look good, and a few true friends are better than the group that's only around for what they think you have. Now this is going to be the most important thing I want you to remember, to truly walk in your feminine power, you have to heal your hurt, from wherever that hurt came from and forgive whoever you need to, I know you are going to say, "I'm not hurting, there is no one I need to forgive." But trust me, it is. Remember this, forgiveness is not for the other person, it's for you so you can heal and get all the blessing that your higher power has for you. Trust me when you do this, you will feel lighter and stand taller than you will ever know. Your feminine power comes from all of this, everything else is just icing on the cake!

RELATIONSHIP WITH PEOPLE

Hey Ladybugs, these last set of letters will be about relationships with people, I chose to close with this because we meet a lot of people in our lifetime and some well all of them are sent to us during seasons in our lives, we just have to be able to know when that season ends or if their season with us last for a lifetime. We must remember that we are the ones that set the tone for every relationship that we encounter with every person in our lives. So as the great poet, Maya Angelou, said, "When a person shows you who they are, believe them the first time." See one thing that I've had to learn about the people I have encountered in my life is that they can never take the same pain that they inflicted on you when it comes back to them. So, sometimes it's best to step outside of yourself and let your higher power handle what you can't and trust that he or she will make it so the person that wronged you will either experience that same situation so they can see what it was like for you or the Higher power of your over standing will have them experience life issues to where they may have to come back and ask for your help.

Heyy lady,

Today is the first day of relationships with people, "Always know that you are not everybody's cup of tea"-Kerry Lite

This means, as much as you want everyone to love who you are many won't. And I know you are saying, "What's not to like about me?", and in reality it might not be anything, people have their own way of judging people. I want you to remember this one important thang; "How a person feels about you has nothing at all to do with you". It's all personal, and nine times out of ten, the flaw that they see in you, they have the same exact flaw.

Heyy girl, how you doin?

It's day two of relationships with people. Today, I want you to know your worth, and trust me when you do, you will not tolerate any nonsense from anyone. You are never anyone's second, you should always come first and demand as much. This is about self-respect in a relationship and your self-respect is the most important part of being who you are!

Heyy love,

Today is day three of relationships with people. Today, I want you to know that people will notice how you are acting differently, but won't notice the behavior they had that caused your change. So by saying this means, a person will only do to you what you allow them to do. When you start to set your boundaries, you are "acting different," as you should, because people didn't respect you as you were, so now they don't know why you are acting "funny," but they never took into account what they said or did was the reason you had to put up those boundaries in the first place. So, keep your values HIGH on how people should treat you, because if you don't, it will keep you in a fog!!

Heyy baby girl.

Today is day four of us talking about relationships with people. Listen, I want you to over stand this, never take unfair criticisms to heart. Remember, " that people see your actions and motives through their own lenses, and sometimes their lenses are scratched by the harsh experiences they've endured" - Rigel Dawson.

As the old saying goes, hurt people hurt people. So what I have learned is that when someone close to you, friend or family member, goes out of their way to say or do something to hurt you, remember this. "The things they don't like about you are actually the things they don't like about themselves, and the way a person feels about you has nothing to do with you"

Heyy girl,

This is day five of relationships and people. This quote your granny used to say, and it still holds true today, "everybody is not your friend!! Just because they hang around you and laugh with you doesn't mean they are your friend." Now you must remember, people pretend very well, but at the end of the day, "real situations expose fake people," so keep your eyes open. You know the saying, "A wolf in sheep's clothing," they have hidden agendas!! So you have to always be aware of those who are in your circle, remember to listen to your gut!! If the person is not right, they are not right!!

Heyy sweetie,

Today is day six of relationships and people. Just for today, I want you to remember this: "Never compare your life to others, there's no comparison between the sun and the moon, they shine when it's their time." -Christopher Ferrel

So, stay in your lane, work hard, and believe with certainty that your time is coming and it's just for you. Your light will shine bright when it's supposed to. Remember, "The brightest lights shine through the darkest of nights".

Heyy ladybug!!

Today is the last day we are talking about relationships and people, so I'm going to end with this quote, "I want you to not worry about those who talk about you behind your back; they are behind you for a reason." The people that fall by the wayside and become part of your past just means that your season with them has ended. One thing that I have learned about true friends and loved ones is that no matter how much time has passed by, when you see them or you hear their voice on the phone, it's like you have never missed a beat. You pick up right where you left off, those are the true ones, the ones that you keep near and dear to your heart. Remember ladies, time and space may get in the way of connecting with the ones you hold close, but the memories, stories, and laughs will keep you together a lifetime.

FINAL INSPIRATION

Ladies, I want to leave you with these tidbits, No matter how big or small we all need a word or phrase to help us get over the humps of life, So read these words and let them soak in, and use them whenever you need that extra push!!

Pretty girl, continue to be BOLD and walk in your PERSONIFIED FEMININITY, loving all there is to love about the most critical person- You!!! And to the WARRIOR WOMAN, continue to stand firm and teach other women to know their worth and intercede for your sistas with your words of wisdom when they need strength! And to the little girl that still lives inside of us-take your shoes off and DANCE in the rain like nobody's watching!! Continue to love the you that you are becoming. It's all a process. Always take the time to work on you and never let anyone put a damper on your Shine!!

Remember, when things get hard, and trust me they will, it's all a process. One of the most precious things is made when pressure is applied, a DIAMOND!! So take it one day at a time and know it might look hazy, but the sun is always going to shine!!! I want you to write this down and put it up so you can see it every day; WHEN GOD IS FOR YOU, WHO CAN BE AGAINST YOU??

Finally, ladies I want you to read these letters, then write your thoughts out when you feel the need in the pages that follow. I want you to write this quote of mine and put it so you can see it every day, "YOU CAN NEVER PUT A LIMIT ON DETERMINATION!"

Ladies, I'm leaving you with this, when you wake up and jump outta your bed and after you thank God for another day ,ask this question aloud, "WHO WOULD I BE TO DENY MYSELF OF ANY GOOD THANG?" (And that's anything that you feel you deserve).

Journal

_____

_____

_____

_____

_____

_____

_____

_____

_____

_____

_____

_____

_____

_____

Journal

_____

_____

_____

_____

_____

_____

_____

_____

_____

_____

_____

_____

_____

_____

Journal

_____

_____

_____

_____

_____

_____

_____

_____

_____

_____

_____

_____

_____

_____

_____

_____

Journal

_____

_____

_____

_____

_____

_____

_____

_____

_____

_____

_____

_____

_____

_____

Journal

_____

_____

_____

_____

_____

_____

_____

_____

_____

_____

_____

_____

_____

_____

Journal

_____

_____

_____

_____

_____

_____

_____

_____

_____

_____

_____

_____

_____

_____

_____

Journal

_____

_____

_____

_____

_____

_____

_____

_____

_____

_____

_____

_____

_____

_____

_____

_____

Journal

_____

_____

_____

_____

_____

_____

_____

_____

_____

_____

_____

_____

_____

_____

Journal

_____

_____

_____

_____

_____

_____

_____

_____

_____

_____

_____

_____

_____

_____

_____

_____

Journal

_____

_____

_____

_____

_____

_____

_____

_____

_____

_____

_____

_____

_____

_____

_____

Journal

_____

_____

_____

_____

_____

_____

_____

_____

_____

_____

_____

_____

_____

Journal

_____

_____

_____

_____

_____

_____

_____

_____

_____

_____

_____

_____

_____

_____

Journal

_____

_____

_____

_____

_____

_____

_____

_____

_____

_____

_____

_____

_____

_____

Journal

_____

_____

_____

_____

_____

_____

_____

_____

_____

_____

_____

_____

_____

_____

_____

Journal

_____

_____

_____

_____

_____

_____

_____

_____

_____

_____

_____

_____

_____

_____

_____

Journal

_____

_____

_____

_____

_____

_____

_____

_____

_____

_____

_____

_____

_____

_____

Journal

_____

_____

_____

_____

_____

_____

_____

_____

_____

_____

_____

_____

_____

_____

Journal

Journal

_____

_____

_____

_____

_____

_____

_____

_____

_____

_____

_____

_____

_____

_____

Journal

_____

_____

_____

_____

_____

_____

_____

_____

_____

_____

_____

_____

_____

_____

_____

Journal

_____

_____

_____

_____

_____

_____

_____

_____

_____

_____

_____

_____

_____

_____

_____

Journal

_____

_____

_____

_____

_____

_____

_____

_____

_____

_____

_____

_____

_____

_____

Journal

_____

_____

_____

_____

_____

_____

_____

_____

_____

_____

_____

_____

_____

_____

Journal

_____

_____

_____

_____

_____

_____

_____

_____

_____

_____

_____

_____

_____

Journal

Journal

_____

_____

_____

_____

_____

_____

_____

_____

_____

_____

_____

_____

_____

_____

_____

_____

Journal

Journal

_____

_____

_____

_____

_____

_____

_____

_____

_____

_____

_____

_____

_____

_____

_____

_____

Journal

_____

_____

_____

_____

_____

_____

_____

_____

_____

_____

_____

_____

_____

_____

_____

_____

Journal

Journal

_____

_____

_____

_____

_____

_____

_____

_____

_____

_____

_____

_____

_____

_____

_____

_____

_____

Journal

Journal

_____

_____

_____

_____

_____

_____

_____

_____

_____

_____

_____

_____

_____

Journal

_____

_____

_____

_____

_____

_____

_____

_____

_____

_____

_____

_____

_____

_____

Journal

_____

_____

_____

_____

_____

_____

_____

_____

_____

_____

_____

_____

_____

Journal

Journal

_____

_____

_____

_____

_____

_____

_____

_____

_____

_____

_____

_____

_____

_____

_____

Journal

_____

_____

_____

_____

_____

_____

_____

_____

_____

_____

_____

_____

_____

_____

_____

_____

Journal

_____

_____

_____

_____

_____

_____

_____

_____

_____

_____

_____

_____

_____

Journal

Journal

_____

_____

_____

_____

_____

_____

_____

_____

_____

_____

_____

_____

_____

_____

Journal

_____

_____

_____

_____

_____

_____

_____

_____

_____

_____

_____

_____

_____

_____

Journal

_____

_____

_____

_____

_____

_____

_____

_____

_____

_____

_____

_____

_____

_____

_____

Journal

_____

_____

_____

_____

_____

_____

_____

_____

_____

_____

_____

_____

_____

_____

_____

Journal

_____

_____

_____

_____

_____

_____

_____

_____

_____

_____

_____

_____

_____

_____

_____

_____

Journal

Journal

_____

_____

_____

_____

_____

_____

_____

_____

_____

_____

_____

_____

_____

_____

Journal

_____

_____

_____

_____

_____

_____

_____

_____

_____

_____

_____

_____

_____

_____

Journal

_____

_____

_____

_____

_____

_____

_____

_____

_____

_____

_____

_____

_____

_____

Journal

_____

_____

_____

_____

_____

_____

_____

_____

_____

_____

_____

_____

_____

CPSIA information can be obtained
at www.ICGtesting.com
Printed in the USA
BVHW041059221022
649859BV00002B/79